WOMEN IN SCIENCE

CHIEN-SHIUNG WU

Phenomenal Physicist

Jill C. Wheeler

ABDO Publishing Company

visit us at
www.abdopublishing.com

Printed in the United States of America, North Mankato, Minnesota.
052012
092012

 PRINTED ON RECYCLED PAPER

Cover Photos: AIP Emilio Segrè Visual Archives; Thinkstock
Interior Photos: AIP Emilio Segrè Visual Archives p. 17; AIP Emilio Segrè Visual Archives,
    Physics Today Collection pp. 5, 6; AIP Emilio Segrè Visual Archives, Segrè Collection p. 13;
    AP Images pp. 7, 9, 11; Corbis p. 23; Getty Images pp. 21, 25, 27; Granger Collection p. 19;
    iStockphoto p. 15; Photo Researchers p. 15

Series Coordinator: BreAnn Rumsch
Editors: Megan M. Gunderson, BreAnn Rumsch
Art Direction: Neil Klinepier

Library of Congress Cataloging-in-Publication Data

Wheeler, Jill C., 1964-
  Chien-Shiung Wu : phenomenal physicist / Jill C. Wheeler.
      p. cm. -- (Women in science)
  Includes index.
  ISBN 978-1-61783-451-6
  1. Wu, C. S. (Chien-shiung), 1912-1997. 2. Physicists--Biography--Juvenile literature. 3. Women physicists--Biography--Juvenile literature. 4. Chinese Americans--Biography--Juvenile literature. I. Title.
  QC16.W785W54 2013
  530.92--dc23
  [B]
                                    2012011515

CONTENTS

CHIEN-SHIUNG WU

> "I have always felt that in physics, and probably in other endeavors too, you must have total commitment. It is not just a job. It is a way of life."
>
> — *Chien-Shiung Wu*

Chien-Shiung Wu is among the most respected female scientists in US history. During her career, she made major contributions to **nuclear physics**. Wu was one of the most talented research scientists ever to work in that field.

Although she found success, Wu still faced **discrimination** during much of her career. Out of this struggle, she became a pioneer for women in science. Wu's life was not always easy. But, she worked hard and overcame great odds.

Today, Wu is a role model for people both inside and outside the world of science. Her many successes have inspired women scientists around the world to chase their dreams.

CHANGES IN CHINA

Chien-Shiung Wu was born on May 31, 1912, in the small town of Liuhe near Shanghai, China. She was the second of Wu Zhongyi and Fan Funhua's three children. Chien-Shiung had an older and a younger brother.

During Chien-Shiung's childhood, China experienced much change. The Chinese Revolution had begun in 1911.

Chien-Shiung's father had taken part in the uprising. The revolution ended a long history of rule by **dynasties**.

After the revolution, most Chinese people still believed men and women were not equal. Public education for girls was discouraged. Women could become housewives, teachers, or nurses.

After leaving China, Chien-Shiung wore Chinese clothing and ate Chinese foods. These efforts helped her stay connected to her home.

In 2011, China celebrated 100 years since the Chinese Revolution of 1911.

Chien-Shiung's father did not agree with this belief system. Zhongyi had learned about equal rights for women. He believed education was important for both boys and girls. This belief would change his daughter's life.

EARLY INSPIRATION

Zhongyi was determined to turn his beliefs into action. Soon after the revolution, he quit his job as an engineer. Then, he opened the Mingde school. It was one of China's first schools to allow girls. Chien-Shiung was allowed to attend.

Like her father, Chien-Shiung's mother also supported equal rights. Her mother was proud of Zhongyi's work. She visited local families and asked them to allow their daughters to attend Mingde.

Chien-Shiung loved school. But she was also inspired to learn at home. The house was filled with books, magazines, and newspapers. Chien-Shiung learned early on to love reading and discovering new things. The family often read together. And Zhongyi always encouraged his children to ask questions, solve problems, and think for themselves.

Thanks to her father's support, Chien-Shiung (second from right) was able to follow her dreams to success. In 1946, Mademoiselle magazine named her one of four "Young Women of the Year."

LESSONS AT SCHOOL

The Mingde school only offered four grades. So, young Chien-Shiung graduated at just nine years old. Yet she wasn't ready to stop learning! The family decided she must continue her education.

The Soochow School for Girls was one of the finest schools available. Chien-Shiung passed the entrance examination. But, the school was about 50 miles (80 km) away in Suzhou. She would have to live there.

The Soochow School had two parts. There was an academic school and the Normal School. The Normal School prepared students to be teachers. Chien-Shiung attended the Normal School because it was free.

In 1922, Chien-Shiung left home. At school, she quickly realized something. She was much more interested in what her friends in the academic school were learning. She wanted to learn these things too! So, Chien-Shiung borrowed their math and science textbooks to study on her own.

While studying, Chien-Shiung learned about Marie Curie. Curie was famous for her pioneering research on **radioactivity**.

Chien-Shiung felt inspired. Now she knew she did not want to teach children. She wanted to study **physics**!

Marie Curie discovered the element radium.

STUDYING SCIENCE

Wu graduated from Soochow's Normal School in 1930. She received the highest grades in her class. At just 17 years old, it was time for her to go to college.

That summer, Wu was selected to attend National Central University in Nanjing, China. Instead of being excited about this news, she was worried. Wu knew she wanted to study **physics**. However, she did not yet know enough mathematics. She feared she would have to be a teacher after all.

Wu's father wanted to support his daughter's dreams. So he gave her books on mathematics, physics, and other sciences. Wu was thrilled and began studying right away!

In her first year of college, Wu focused on mathematics. When she felt she had enough of these skills, she turned her focus to physics.

Wu's name reflects her family's will for the life she would lead. **Chien-Shiung** *means "courageous hero."*

All of Wu's hard work paid off. In 1934, she finished college at the top of her class. She was grateful for her father's support. She believed that without it she would have been a schoolteacher in China.

CHANGE OF PLANS

After college, Wu taught **physics** at Zhejiang University in Hangzhou. One year later, she became a researcher at Academia Sinica's Institute of Physics in Shanghai.

At her new job, Wu met Jinghui Gu. Gu had earned her **PhD** in the United States. Wu was inspired. She decided to earn a PhD, too. But she knew this would mean leaving home. At the time, China did not offer a PhD in physics.

Gu suggested that Wu study at the University of Michigan–Ann Arbor. So in August 1936, Wu boarded a ship bound for the United States. Her goal was to earn her PhD and then return to China.

Wu's first stop in the United States was San Francisco, California. While there, she visited the nearby University of California–Berkeley (Cal). Wu found out that Ernest Lawrence taught there. He was one of the world's leading physicists. Now Wu was interested in attending Cal.

During her visit, Wu met a student named Luke Chia-Liu Yuan. They discovered they had much in common. He was also a physics student from China. Their talk swayed Wu to attend Cal instead of Michigan.

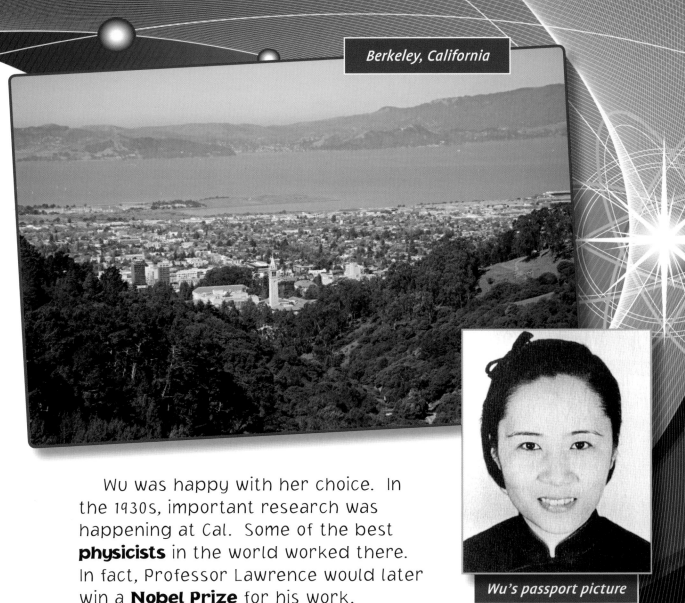

Wu was happy with her choice. In the 1930s, important research was happening at Cal. Some of the best **physicists** in the world worked there. In fact, Professor Lawrence would later win a **Nobel Prize** for his work.

Wu's passport picture

15

DR. WU

At Cal, Wu was excited to learn as much as possible. Yet this was also a difficult time for her. Years earlier, Japanese soldiers had invaded China. As a result, Wu had lost all contact with her family. She would not hear from them again until 1945.

Wu worried about her family. But she also remembered her father's advice. He had said to "ignore the obstacles. Just put your head down and keep walking forward." So she did.

Wu's professors were brilliant **physicists** such as J. Robert Oppenheimer, Enrico Fermi, and Emilio Segrè. These men quickly recognized Wu's hard work and sharp mind. She was able to work with them on their **nuclear** physics research.

In 1940, Wu completed her **PhD**. She stayed on at Cal's lab as a research assistant for two more years. She continued to earn respect as an expert there.

In 1942, Wu was ready for a new adventure. On May 30, she and Yuan married. Shortly after, they moved to the East Coast.

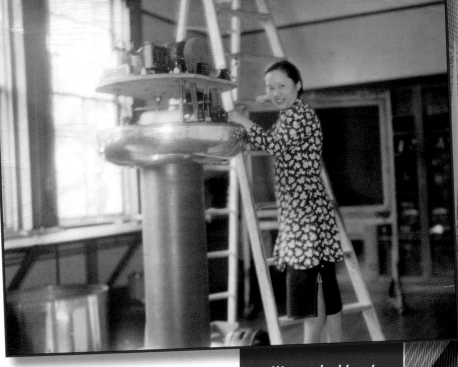

Next, Wu began teaching at Smith College in Northampton, Massachusetts. A year later, she became the first female instructor at Princeton University in New Jersey.

Wu worked hard as a student. As a teacher, she expected the same from her students.

The Manhattan Project

>> *J. Robert Oppenheimer served as director of the Manhattan Project.*

Wu's work at Princeton was cut short by **World War II**. In March 1944, she was asked to join the top secret Manhattan Project in New York. There, work was underway at the Division of War Research at Columbia University. The US Army was developing an **atomic bomb**.

Wu accepted the position and moved to New York City. She proved to be an important team member. She took part in developing **radiation** detectors. And, her research at Berkeley helped the scientists learn how to make large amounts of uranium 235. This was the special fuel needed for the bomb.

In August 1945, the army was ready to use its secret weapon. Two atomic bombs were dropped on Japan. These measures ended the war.

The United States dropped the atomic bomb "Little Boy" (right) on Hiroshima on August 6. It dropped a second bomb on Nagasaki on August 9.

Workers created the materials for the first atomic bomb at the Oak Ridge plant in Tennessee (above). Wu's research aided this work.

19

MORE OPPORTUNITIES

After the war, Wu was finally able to contact her family. She told them about everything she had done in America. Then in 1947, Wu became a mother. She and her husband named their son Vincent Wei-chen Yuan. Like his parents, he would become a **physicist**.

In the late 1940s, Wu and her husband were asked to teach at China's National Central University. This would mean a return home. However, China had a **communist** government by then. So, the couple decided to remain in the United States. They became US citizens in 1954.

By then, Wu had also returned to her career. In late 1945, she became a research associate at Columbia University. From 1946 to 1952, Wu focused on a form of **radioactivity** known as beta decay. She studied how unstable atoms become more stable by giving off energy.

In 1952, Wu was named an associate professor at Columbia. And, she continued working in the lab. She was known for her careful approach to experiments.

Dr. Ernest Ambler (right) *shared Wu's enthusiasm for physics. They worked together on important research.*

LAWS OF NATURE

In 1956, everything changed. Two scientists named Tsung-Dao Lee and Chen Ning Yang came to Wu. They told her they wanted to test the **conservation of parity**. They needed Wu's help.

The law of parity was well accepted by scientists. To question it was similar to doubting the law of gravity! Still, Lee and Yang did not believe the law was correct in all situations.

The men asked Wu to test their theory. She agreed to help. Wu's careful experiments showed that the law was not valid in beta decay. Her work proved Lee and Yang were correct.

The three scientists announced their discovery in 1957. The news shocked scientists everywhere. This changed basic thinking about the structure of the physical world!

In 1957, the **Nobel Prize** in **Physics** was awarded. However, only Lee and Yang were named. Wu's research had broken a barrier in science. But it seemed the barriers women in science faced still held strong.

Wu's experiments were often difficult, but the results could be trusted. Many were carried out with help from graduate students.

AWARDS GALORE

Wu felt let down after not winning the **Nobel Prize**. However, she never quit working. Science was what mattered most to her.

In 1958, Wu became a full professor at Columbia University. That same year, Princeton University granted her an honorary **PhD** in science. She was the first woman to earn this recognition.

The honors did not stop there. That same year, Wu was elected to the National Academy of Sciences (NAS). She became the seventh female member. In 1962, the NAS gave Wu the Cyrus B. Comstock Award.

In 1972, Wu joined the American Academy of Arts and Sciences. Then in 1975, she became the first woman to head the American Physical Society. This is the top US organization for **physicists**.

Also in 1975, Wu received the nation's highest scientific award. President Gerald Ford presented her with the National Medal of Science. And in 1980, Wu received the internationally respected Wolf Prize.

In 1965, Wu published Beta Decay. This book remains a standard source on the topic.

PHYSICS STAR

>> *Wu is the first scientist to have an asteroid named after her while she was still living.*

Even with challenges, Wu led a successful career. It was clear how much other scientists respected her work. Wu spent 37 years at Columbia. Over that time, she explored various laws of **physics** and new types of atoms. She retired in 1981.

Wu had returned to China for the first time in 1973. Following her retirement, she began traveling more. She advised scientists around the world. Wu also spoke out to support equal rights for women in science.

Wu died of a **stroke** on February 16, 1997. She was 84 years old. The following year, Wu earned yet another honor. She was named to the American National Women's Hall of Fame.

The "courageous hero" left behind an inspiring story. She showed what can happen when one ignores the

obstacles and just walks forward. Today, Chien-Shiung Wu is recognized for her many firsts that helped clear a path for women in science. She continues to be a role model and hero to many.

TIMELINE

1912
On May 31, Chien-Shiung Wu was born in Liuhe, China.

1934
Wu graduated from National Central University in Nanjing, China.

1936
In August, Wu traveled to the United States; she became a student at the University of California–Berkeley (Cal).

1940
Wu earned her PhD and worked as a research assistant at Cal.

1944
In March, Wu joined the top secret Manhattan Project to help develop an atomic bomb.

1946
Wu began her research on beta decay.

1956
Wu proved the law of parity does not apply in beta decay; this helped Lee and Yang earn the Nobel Prize in Physics the next year.

1975
President Gerald Ford presented Wu with the National Medal of Science.

1981
Wu retired after 37 years as a researcher at Columbia University in New York City, New York.

1997
Wu died of a stroke on February 16.

DIG DEEPER

Dr. Chien-Shiung Wu understood that everything in physics relates to the physical properties that make up the world we live in. One of the best ways to see these properties in action is by testing Sir Isaac Newton's three laws of motion.

SUPPLIES:
• two rulers • masking tape • a book • a Ping-Pong ball • four marbles

INSTRUCTIONS: *Always ask an adult for help!*

1 Lay both rulers next to each other on a flat, level surface. Leave about 0.25 inches (0.6 cm) between them to create a groove. Then, tape them down to secure in place. Place the book against one end of the groove as a stopper.

2 Newton's first law of motion says that an object at rest will stay at rest until an external force acts upon it. Set a marble in the middle of the groove, at rest. Does anything happen?

3 Newton's first law of motion also says an object in motion will stay in motion until an external force acts upon it. Starting at the open end of the groove, roll a second marble toward the first one. What happens to the first marble? The second?

4 Newton's second law of motion says that when a force acts upon an object, the object moves in the direction of the force. Remove the marbles and the book. Now set one marble and the Ping-Pong ball at opposite ends of the ruler groove. Roll them toward each other at the same speed. What happens when they meet?

5 Newton's third law says that for each action there is an equal and opposite reaction. Remove the Ping-Pong ball and add two marbles, lining up all three in the middle of the groove. Roll a fourth marble toward the others. What happens to the three resting marbles? What happens to the fourth marble? Repeat, but this time roll three marbles toward just one at rest. What happens?

GLOSSARY

atomic bomb – an extremely powerful bomb that uses the energy of atoms.

communist – relating to a social and economic system in which everything is owned by the government and given to the people as needed.

conservation of parity – a physics law stating that two physical systems must behave in identical fashion if one is the mirror image of the other.

discrimination – unfair treatment, often based on race, religion, or gender.

dynasty – a series of rulers who belong to the same family.

Nobel Prize – any of six annual awards given to people who have made the greatest contributions to mankind. The prizes are awarded for physics, chemistry, medicine, economics, literature, and peace.

nuclear – relating to or powered by nuclear energy. Nuclear energy is created when atoms are divided or combined.

PhD – doctor of philosophy. Usually, this is the highest degree a student can earn.

physics – a science that studies matter and energy and how they interact. A scientist who studies physics is a physicist.

radiation – the act or process of giving out light, heat, electricity, or other radiant energy.

radioactivity – the giving off of rays of energy by the breaking apart of atoms of certain elements.

stroke – a sudden loss of sensation, voluntary motion, and mental activity. It is caused by the breaking of a blood vessel in the brain.

World War II – from 1939 to 1945, fought in Europe, Asia, and Africa. Great Britain, France, the United States, the Soviet Union, and their allies were on one side. Germany, Italy, Japan, and their allies were on the other side.

WEB SITES

To learn more about Chien-Shiung Wu, visit ABDO Publishing Company online. Web sites about Chien-Shiung Wu are featured on our Book Links page. These links are routinely monitored and updated to provide the most current information available.

www.abdopublishing.com

INDEX